THE 3RD COMIC BOOK

ESPECIALLY FOR TEENAGERS WITH ASD!

THE GIRL WITH THE CURLY HAIR

HELPING PEOPLE WITH ASPERGER'S SYNDROME AND THEIR LOVED ONES COMMUNICATE

BY ALIS ROWE

Also by Alis Rowe

One Lonely Mind
978-0-9562693-0-0

The Girl with the Curly Hair - Asperger's and Me
978-0-9562693-2-4

The 1st Comic Book
978-0-9562693-1-7

The 2nd Comic Book
978-0-9562693-4-8

Websites:
www.alisrowe.co.uk
www.thegirlwiththecurlyhair.co.uk
www.womensweightlifting.co.uk

Social Media:
www.facebook.com/thegirlwiththecurlyhair
www.twitter.com/curlyhairedalis

THE GIRL WITH THE CURLY HAIR

PRESENTS

THE 3RD COMIC BOOK

ALIS ROWE

Lonely Mind Books
London

Copyrighted Material

First published in 2014
by Lonely Mind Books
London

Copyright © Alis Rowe 2014

Printed and bound in the USA

ISBN 9780956269331

9 780956 269331

For people with Asperger's Syndrome and their Neurotypical families and friends

and

my Facebook friends

hello

With the success of 'The 1st Comic Book' and 'The 2nd Comic Book' it was time to write number three!

The 3rd Comic Book is intended for teenagers and young adults with Asperger's Syndrome, however it will also appeal to older adults, particularly if they think back to their school days.

I hope this book is enjoyed by everyone – in particular parents and teachers. I would like them to see what life is like from a different perspective.

This book is a starting point for discussions between parents, teachers and adolescents/young people. Use the 'space for your notes' pages to talk about how each situation affects you - if it does! It might not - after all, everyone on the spectrum is different.

Best wishes,

Alis aka The Girl with the Curly Hair

Contents

Speed limits

SPACE FOR YOUR NOTES...

THE GIRL WITH THE CURLY HAIR

IS GETTING A LIFT FROM HER FRIEND AND HER FRIEND'S MUM.

IN HER MIND, RULES SHOULD ALWAYS BE FOLLOWED AND NEVER, EVER BENT.

A big bottom

SPACE FOR YOUR NOTES...

THE GIRL WITH THE CURLY HAIR

IS SHOPPING FOR CLOTHES WITH HER FRIEND.

HER HONESTY SOMETIMES UPSETS THE PEOPLE SHE CARES ABOUT MOST.

Trying on clothes

SPACE FOR YOUR NOTES...

THE GIRL WITH THE CURLY HAIR

IS OUT WITH HER NEUROTYPICAL FRIENDS.

IN ORDER TO FEEL PART OF THE GROUP, SHE HAS TO DO THINGS SHE DOESN'T LIKE... BUT SHE HAS HER OWN SOLUTIONS!

IT'S REALLY FUN TRYING ON NEW CLOTHES AND SEEING HOW GOOD YOU CAN LOOK!

MOST OF THE TIME SHE DOESN'T EVEN BUY ANYTHING. WHAT IS THE POINT OF TRYING ON CLOTHES WITHOUT BUYING THEM?

LET'S GO SHOPPING. I WANT TO LOOK AT THE SUMMER DRESSES!

UMM OK. I'LL HOLD YOUR BAG THEN, WHILE YOU TRY THEM ON

Branded trainers

SPACE FOR YOUR NOTES...

Boy friends

SPACE FOR YOUR NOTES...

The Girl with the Curly Hair

Prefers to hang out with boys.

She finds boys easier to talk to, but the girls mistake it for disloyalty.

Drama class

SPACE FOR YOUR NOTES...

THE GIRL WITH THE CURLY HAIR

SOMETIMES PRETENDS TO LIKE WHAT HER FRIENDS LIKE, FOR EXAMPLE DRAMA CLASS.

SHE DESPERATELY WANTS TO FIT IN BUT IS SUPER AWARE THAT SHE DOESN'T.

Dining hall

SPACE FOR YOUR NOTES...

THE GIRL WITH THE CURLY HAIR

IS WITH HER FRIEND LOOKING FOR A TABLE IN THE DINING HALL.

HER FRIEND'S CHOICE OF TABLE IS CERTAINLY NOT HERS.

Art class

SPACE FOR YOUR NOTES...

THE GIRL WITH THE CURLY HAIR

IS IN ART CLASS. THE TEACHER ASKS THE CLASS TO "DRAW SOMETHING FROM IMAGINATION." SHE FINDS THIS VERY HARD WITHOUT A BIT MORE DIRECTION.

School corridor

SPACE FOR YOUR NOTES...

THE GIRL WITH THE CURLY HAIR

IS WALKING TO HER NEXT CLASSROOM.

THE SCHOOL CORRIDORS ARE HORRENDOUSLY STRESSFUL FOR HER.

Tattle-tale

SPACE FOR YOUR NOTES...

THE GIRL WITH THE CURLY HAIR

TELLS THE TEACHER EVERY TIME SOMEONE SWEARS.
SHE DOES NOT UNDERSTAND WHY THIS GETS HER IN TROUBLE.

Doodling

SPACE FOR YOUR NOTES...

The register

SPACE FOR YOUR NOTES...

THE GIRL WITH THE CURLY HAIR

IS WAITING TO BE DISMISSED FOR HOME TIME, BUT THE TEACHER **WON'T LET HER GO.**

THERE ARE SO MANY THINGS STRESSFUL ABOUT THIS.

Desk marks

SPACE FOR YOUR NOTES...

THE GIRL WITH THE CURLY HAIR

IS MAKING MARKS ON HER DESK WITH HER COMPASS.

THE TEACHER'S CHOICE OF PHRASE IS CONFUSING.

A late friend

SPACE FOR YOUR NOTES...

THE GIRL WITH THE CURLY HAIR

HAS ARRANGED TO SEE A FRIEND AT 3PM.

LATENESS MEANS DIFFERENT THINGS TO DIFFERENT PEOPLE.

Sharing sweets

Dehydration

SPACE FOR YOUR NOTES...

The Girl with the Curly Hair

is out cycling with her friend on a hot day.

She feels very distressed by her friend's lack of preparation.

Changing her mind

SPACE FOR YOUR NOTES...

THE GIRL WITH THE CURLY HAIR HAS ARRANGED TO SPEND TIME WITH HER FRIENDS AFTER SCHOOL.

AS THE DAY GOES ON, SHE CHANGES HER MIND AND WORRIES ABOUT IT.

Flirting

SPACE FOR YOUR NOTES...

THE GIRL WITH THE CURLY HAIR

IS WALKING HOME WHEN A BOY FROM HER CLASS APPROACHES HER.

SHE FINDS IT HARD TO READ THE SOCIAL SIGNALS.

Well meaning teacher

SPACE FOR YOUR NOTES...

THE GIRL WITH THE CURLY HAIR

IS TAKEN TO AN EMPTY CLASSROOM TO CALM DOWN.

GRADUALLY HOWEVER, OTHER STUDENTS FILTER IN AND THE TEACHER DOES NOTHING TO STOP THEM.

JUST SIT IN HERE WITH ME FOR A BIT UNTIL YOU FEEL BETTER

I NEEDED TO BE AWAY FROM OTHER PEOPLE, NOT NEAR THEM. TOO MANY NOISES AND SIGHTS. I FEEL OVERWHELMED

SHE'S JUST HAVING A TANTRUM. IF I CAN JUST GET HER BACK TO THE OTHER ROOM SHE'LL BE FINE

WHY DID SHE TELL ME I WOULD HAVE A QUIET SPACE, JUST ME AND HER, AND THEN ALLOW OTHER STUDENTS IN?

IT DOESN'T MATTER IF A FEW OTHERS HAVE COME IN TO SEE WHAT'S GOING ON. THERE'S ONLY THREE OF THEM

SHE BROKE HER WORD. I CAN'T TRUST HER ANYMORE

Group assignment

SPACE FOR YOUR NOTES...

The Girl with the Curly Hair

is in English class. The teacher gives them a group assignment.

Whereas her neurotypical peers seem to enjoy group work, for her there's nothing worse.

Essay

SPACE FOR YOUR NOTES...

THE GIRL WITH THE CURLY HAIR

IS WRITING AN ESSAY. THE END OF DAY SCHOOL BELL GOES.

HER INFLFLEXIBLE THINKING MAKES IT HARD TO LEAVE THINGS UNFINISHED.

The end

Index

Printed in Great Britain
by Amazon.co.uk, Ltd.,
Marston Gate.